Reflections:

A Mythology in Poetry & Prose

Azure Hall

Praise for *Reflections*

"Azure Hall's powerful prose is like a walk in the forest amongst the tallest of trees, her wisdom encouraging me to rise up and not lose sight of myself in this business of living."
— Carine McCandless, Bestelling Author of *The Wild Truth*

"A revelatory and insightful exploration of the self, *Reflections* utilizes elements of mythology to expose the private and personal complexities hidden by everyday experience."
— Brian Castleberry, Author of *Nine Shiny Objects*

"Azure: the color between shrapneled wave and disambiguated ocean blue, nothing so indiscriminate in its palette and rebellion, yet confiding. This author is her namesake, so much as it allows the corpse of remembered prose to reassemble and rearticulate into delicious, sutured form. A language of Grecian myth and sweet madness that rivals only the vesper of a starlit muse, this reflection in metric tongue begins in magical grief and ends in a love letter to her daughter. How could you not find yourself among these pages?"
— Bianca Viñas, Editor of *Lifelines: Rewriting Lives from Inside Out*

"From the very first page, *Reflections* draws the reader close, asking you lean in and join its characters as they walk the path to self-discovery. These stories in poetry and prose bring well-known myths to life, presenting them in a way that bridges the gap between the individual and the collective. The author's knowledge of the classics and mastery of her craft are clear, and the end result is a wonder."
— Cameron Cobb, Editor in Chief of Joint Special Operations University Press

"Azure has a remarkable ability to capture the raw essence of women's experiences and delve into the depths of complex emotions. This collection offers a profoundly relatable journey through femininity and self-reflection. A beautifully written collection of stories that has left me feeling empowered and inspired."
— Isabella Jannette, Author of *Your Name*

Edited by Flor Ana Mireles

1st Edition | 01
Paperback ISBN: 979-8-9890939-7-7

First Published November 2023

For inquiries and bulk orders, please email:
indieearthbooks@gmail.com

Printed in the United States of America   1 2 3 4 5 6 7 8 9

Indie Earth Publishing Inc.
| Miami, FL |

www.indieearthbooks.com

INDIE EARTH
PUBLISHING

Dedication:

This nonsense is dedicated to the chorus of powerful women in my life who refuse to remain derivative, you taught me to fly.

And to my daughter, may you always remember that your ribs are your own and your narrative is in your hands.

Author's Note:

Before you begin, please understand that this is by no means intended to be an anthology of myths or the women who live on within them. There are countless tales of strong, brave women stemming from cultures across the globe and I would be a fool to assume to see myself in them all.

Rather, this is a personal view of feminine characters and archetypes that impacted my own identity when viewed through the lens of a cisgendered, white woman with barely 30 years under her belt. Their stories are superimposed on my own, and therefore do not follow the myths loyally. I have rewritten endings and taken liberties galore.

I started writing *Reflections* in an attempt to understand myself through literature, to pinpoint the stories that built me and my perceived place in the world. What started to take shape, seemingly by its own accord in a rapidly deteriorating composition notebook, was a string of allegorical reflections that formed the bones of the book you're holding. Once this journal on a serious ego trip was finished, I was left with a sort of coming-of-age collage. A collection of defining moments contextualized within the lines of Homer, Sappho, and even—often begrudgingly—King James. My own personal mythology in 30 pieces.

The nature of my writing and research resulted in a focus on a fragmented selection of mythological ladies I was lucky enough to meet in a life spent reading. Let's say they are the ones who I would invite into my home for a book club. In this context, they help me tell the stories that shaped me—both my own life experiences and those belonging to people I love. These women are my friends and my inspiration, and I hope that they go on to become yours as well. We have plenty of empty seats at book club.

Azure Hall

"May I write words more naked than flesh,
stronger than bone, more resilient than
sinew, sensitive than nerve."

- Sappho

Table of Contents

Reflections

A Quick Note to Krystal at the Cafe

Gather up the scraps of you, my girl.
The battered and beaten golden rays,
the fragments
with their jagged edges.

Though the holding
may be painful,
though you will seep sweet crimson,
the healing will come.

Hold your shards close.
Grip them in a mighty fist.
Let the pain seep through the gaps
in your strong fingers.

And when,
finally,
you own the agony,
let go.

You may worry away
those sharp corners,
or one day find all the ways
in which your angles fit perfectly inside.

On those bright mornings
when the sunlight peeks through your
remaining fissures, remember,
you are born in the breaking.

Arachne's Lament

I decided a long time ago to never again fall victim to sweet words that melt into acid. Never again leave my soft underbelly exposed. Never again be caught unawares, approached from behind or backed into a corner. To be bitten, to have my body broken and my heart tooth torn. To endure just to be swallowed and spat out by my own species. Never again would I allow my divine majesty to be scorned without punishment.

After the last time my heart was ripped from my chest, I ran and poured out all the pain. I heaved and wretched it from the empty place in my middle. Gathered it up in shaking hands, stretched it across the brittle frame of myself, and set to work at the loom.

I shook with sobs that unspooled what was done to me. I spun a lifetime of discontinuous devotion into wisps of hair-thin thread. I wept in warps and wefts and wove myself into something new. Burning basketweaves of betrayal snaked through my very base pairs to create something altogether unknown. I swallowed the stale sugar of false promises to form a backbone and stepped out from behind my Bayeux a victor, venomous and in search of spoils. Spiders eat spiders, you see.

Now a master weaver, I tried my hand at other art forms. I learned to paint myself in miniature, shrinking small as an ant and half as threatening. I sculpted serene smiles, lips curved into contrived coyness to conceal a mouth full of fangs. I plucked sticky heartstring chords with every calculated movement. I sent shivers from my place at the center and vibrated vulnerability. I affected and embodied inescapable entanglement. I never hesitated to strike first, not even once.

The jukebox whispered Willie and Johnny and June while, hunched over pitchers of pale ale, you rushed headlong toward your fate. Your glassy gray eyes met mine and I found in them an eagerness that promised to make light of my labor. It should have stopped there. *I should have stopped it there.* But you were so sure I was caught in your web. And I was so hungry.

That first night, I let you circle. You laid a lacy lattice before me like an orb-weaver and spread your home between two tall oak trees to invite me in. I played my part well, a winged thing waiting to be wrapped up in someone, broken and begging to be bound. I sat and let you decide on your own to draw near. But I didn't have to wait long.

You came when I called. And came when I didn't. You knew the right words to say. And when to say nothing at all. You held me in tanned arms and poured yourself into me, so certain there was space for you. I watched and came to hope there was a scrap of self-preservation in you. That you were playacting along with me. It breaks my heart that, even then, I knew you weren't.

You met me there in the middle, all underbelly and exposure, and loved the fringed thing you found. There were no detours of deceit in your DNA. Unlike mine, the spirals of you held only devotion. I fasted and watched as my prey began to look a lot less like food. You looked like something to be savored. You looked like something to be saved.

I left you in our forest and returned to a lonely loom, determined to weave a new ending into the threads of our fate. Maybe the Moirai would grant an exception, just this once. I wiped away layers of dust and time. I twisted the smooth spindle with the light touch of my thumb and wove a warning into the tapestry of us. "My love, be moderate. Allay your ecstasy," it begged of you. Europa again deceived; my prayer of supplication was refused.

So, I returned with you to your bed of strings and tried to lay still in its center. Tried to assume the character I had so long affected. Exposed myself once again and stayed with you there. I gave you a bundle wrapped in silky thread, a spiderling to bind us together. But it seems that in the course of love, none of us should see salvation.

Layers of balm applied to fresh wounds have left me oil slick. Slippery self-care stops me from sticking to the mesh trappings of a man, even when he deserves it. Restless legs led me to jump. And I did. My safety net was ready and waiting while your back was turned, our baby cradled in your arms. I fell from the height of our home, hungry and alone. Left to live, but live hanging.

Grief is a Thing with Scales

If Hope is a thing with feathers,
Grief is a thing with scales
that snakes around the soul,
squeezes tight, and never stops *at all.*

Left to his own devices,
like Saturn with his sons,
gluttonous Grief will feast on Hope,
leaving not a crumb.

In mourning, you may be tempted,
as many a man has been,
to reach for mirrored shield and sword
to kill the beast within.

Lay your weapons down, my girl;
do not be misled.
Grief is not a gorgon;
you must let him keep his head.

Nor is Grief a dragon,
waiting to be slain.
Consider instead the cobra,
willing to be tamed.

Grief and I became fast friends.
My charms they did prevail
when I tempted him to turn his head
and press his teeth to tail.

After I coaxed him from his basket,
and stilled his snapping jaw,
I asked him, please, to stay awhile,
and help our heart to thaw.

I overwintered an orphan
in his ouroboros embrace
and learned to love the salty tears
that slithered down our face...

'Til Grief and I, we found him,
in the shade of dogwood trees,
and in the seaside sunsets
that brought me to my knees.

I found him in my forehead lines,
and in his favorite books.
Good Grief, my guide, he showed me
all the secret spots to look.

With time, I saw him everywhere,
in nearly every thing.
And feathered Hope returned to roost
in the warmth of this new spring.

Grief, he didn't mind it;
he left the bird to rest.
And even shared the scales he'd shed
to help her build her nest.

Once Upon a Time,

There was a little girl who lived in a haunted house on a hill. But her house didn't start out haunted; haunted houses rarely do.

There was a time when she lived there with her father and theirs was a world of wonder. Its rooms were filled with books and bonsai trees, black and white ballet photography, and the occasional snoozing barn cat, brought home in a backpack after a flash of big eyes and a bit of begging.

Together, this family of two made the house on the hill a home. It seemed as though they would live there forever, picking pears from the tree outside and baking them into pies. But the girl's father was old.

One day, she came home to find that his heart had stopped beating. She sat waiting, certain that hers would follow suit and the two of them would build a new home together in the next place. But inexplicably, it kept on going. More inexplicably still, the world kept on spinning, and she soon found herself with another family.

A beautiful queen came to live in the house on the hill and brought with her two young daughters. The girl was thrilled to have a mother, and the three sisters made plans for a life of splendor, mirth, and good cheer. The house was pleased to be full once again and the girl felt that only love could follow. But she knew nothing of what the future would hold; little girls rarely do.

As the queen unpacked her boxes of dresses and dishes, something else moved in with them. Placing plates and cups in cabinets, she laid shadows by their side. The heavy lace of her curtains left no space for sunlight to stream through and the windows behind seemed covered in ash.

They were surrounded. The queen's angry screams and the girls' resulting cries took the form of ghostly wails that snaked up and down the stairwell. The house did what it could to keep the darkness at bay. It echoed and amplified the infrequent laughter. It breathed out heat on cold winter nights when small feet poked out of blankets. The hinges on the front door sprung open on golden mornings to call them out into the sunlight. But there is only so much a house can do, and a life lived locked indoors took its toll on the girls.

Cloaked in constant shadow, the gold of their hair turned to brass. Their sun-kissed skin first went pale, then grayed. They learned to lower their laughter and speak only in whispers, lest the queen come to extinguish their joy. Still, the girls did what they could to bring forth the light.

They huddled in the attic in the late hours of the night, calling on the old goddesses. They begged Athena and Hecate to grant them the strength to survive. Placing their palms over the flame of a single candle, they learned to hold pain in their hand without fear. They carved symbols for protection into bars of ivory soap and smuggled them into the bath. They snuck out through cracked windows and made their way down to the marsh at the edge of their land, standing still as reeds and looking up to the stars for guidance. They huddled and chanted and grew strong, storing their secrets in a book of spells that they hid below the floorboards.

In the face of this defiant unity, the queen devised new ways to bring them to their knees.

For the eldest daughter, the punishment came as a new pain that the candlelight lessons could not have prepared her for. Her body broke and her heart wasn't far behind. She carved new spells into her skin with razorblades, runes meant to thicken it and shield her heart until neither could be touched. Her sisters memorized the sounds of her screams.

For the youngest daughter, the pain passed over her flesh and went instead for her mind. The queen took her memories and warped them into something unrecognizable to her. She planted seeds of doubt that blossomed into flowers of fear. The little sister lost her faith in reality and no longer considered herself a reliable witness to her own life. Afraid of misspeaking, she learned spells to seal her lips until not even whispers could escape. Her sisters mourned the missing sound of her voice.

For the middle daughter, the lifelong resident of the house on the hill, the queen aimed her wrath at both body and mind. The girl's plate at the dinner table was laid bare and the queen twisted the image in her bedroom mirror into something great and terrible. The insistent, feathery turnings of her stomach were malignant at night. In the darkness, she saw herself growing large and beastly. The growling of her monstrous hunger kept her awake until the morning, filling her days with fatigue. Rather than rest, she wrote her way through those late hours, spinning spells of rage and vengeance in a grimoire all her own. Her sisters repeated her incantations in their dreams.

Worst of all, the queen slashed her sword through the sisters' tethering threads. She fed them scraps of love on the tips of daggers, slitting their tongues and leaving them serpentine. She wove webs of lies that tangled around the girls' slender ankles and bound them to her alone. And when she cast her single golden apple of affection at their feet, the girls scratched and clawed one another until their once-fair faces were lost. At the end of the fight, the sisters had only a single eye and a single tooth left between them. Finally, they were as hideous as she was. But, by this time, the queen was old.

One day, the three sisters woke to find that her heart had stopped beating. And they couldn't be certain, but it felt as though theirs had all started again. It seemed possible that they could build a new home together in the next place. Inexplicably, they kept on going. More inexplicably still, the world kept on spinning. The house exhaled as the three sisters pried up the floorboards and resumed those old, familiar spells of unity.

The girls grew up together, free from the witch's cruel hands. They went on to start families of their own, filling closets and cabinets with the love they were denied.

Some say that the three sisters still wear those old scars, that they still share a single eye and a single tooth between them. But in this new life, they gladly pass the eye when needed. They rest easy, knowing that one will always be awake and watching. And when something comes along in life that is too big to eat on their own, they hand the tooth off to another who can break it into bite-size pieces. Time has made them light as sea foam.

On some dark nights, the howling wind carries with it whispers of the queen's quiet rage. Her old wounds reach their ears as her ghost tries again to unwind the ties that bind them. But the goddesses prepared them for this, too.

For the eldest daughter, the protection comes in the form of tight embraces with her children. Their tiny hands write new runes of hope and forgiveness, and she has taught them to love gently. Her sisters now bottle her tears of happiness.

For the youngest daughter, the truth passes over her lips, and she owns it. She speaks her piece and summons her peace. When her children share their fears and desires, she feeds their minds with affirmations and affection at the end of a silver spoon. Her sisters now know her stories.

For the middle daughter, the only remaining resident of the house on the hill, the beast in her belly fuels further furious writing that reduces the queen's reign to a single chapter. She eats golden apples with her daughter and the pair bake them into pies. And while she still doesn't sleep much, should the old fluttering return, her sisters now wake her from her nightmares.

Paradise Misplaced

You won't find the Garden of Eden
pressed between Old Testament pages.
And it certainly isn't on any map.
But it hasn't been lost either.

It belongs to the little girls now, you see.
The path back to Paradise waits
in the periphery of summer sunshine squints.
If only you know how to find it.

It is dense.
And it is overgrown.
But it is there.
And it is theirs alone.

An invisible queendom
where they slip away from
bedtimes and bathtimes
and the business of growing up.

To a grassy, green glen;
where blades reach up
for tight hugs between twin thumbs
and to be taught to whistle.

Through mud puddle lawns,
they stomp; they revel and romp,
in sloshing, sticky sneakers
that leave ley lines in their wake.

It is for them that the battle drum beats.
Its merry melodies and maypole blooms
bring beautiful battalions on quick feet
that stamp the field in fairy rings.

They dig their hands into the earth.
Clay cakes the carefully clipped cuticles
of nervous mother manicures and
chips away at layers of pretty, pink paint.

Hangnails slice like scythes
through dandelion stems.
Milky white sap rises to the surface,
seeping into the nail beds' topsoil.

Making ten crescent mud-moons
of pirate treasure to secure the flowers
safe passage to puckered lips
and what lies beyond.

Breath-breezes lift achenes from blowballs.
Floating between Eden's inhabitants;
these messengers of Juneau in miniature
carry notes of hope and freedom.

Artemis, too, has made a home
for herself in Paradise,
the only grownup granted
access to their garden.

She watches over those who love noise
and roam up and down through woodlands.
Lends her voice to the chorus of calls
to one another in girlish birdsong.

She dances alongside her sea of nymphs
through tall grass and on steep rock edges.
Blankets this tiny army in arrow-feathered freedom,
her bow aimed and at the ready.

Poised to strike down the unseen dangers
that lurk and linger just beyond the border.
But even the devoted care of this mighty huntress
only serves to delay the inevitable.

For each of these sinewy soldiers,
the time will come when Eden is lost to them, too.
There is no escaping the brand of banishment
burned onto their very bones at first bite.

Before tree-fruit can tame growling bellies,
the view from the Garden has changed.
Shadows stretch hungry hands to reach for you.
Roses seem strangled by their own thorny stems.

The path back to Paradise warps
and begins to look a little too dark,
too winding, for a girl to travel alone.
It probably is best to head home.

Return to the safety of deadbolts,
bedtimes,
bathtimes,
and the business of growing up.

Artemis alone remains,
tending the Garden in your absence.
Patiently waiting for the next row of troops
to arrive and lead the crusade.

A Common Procedure

Aphrodite was getting ready for the first day of seventh grade when they came for her. A group of men in white lab coats pushed open the door to her bedroom and spilled in. They were impossibly tall behind her stool at the pink Barbie vanity. One of the men grabbed her by the wrist and led her from her home like a sacrificial lamb. Grass sprouted and died with each of her steps down the path.

When Aphrodite woke, she was laid flat on a metal table, bound in a net that pressed squares into her pale flesh and held her to the cold surface. Naked, aside from a frog-print training bra and matching panties, she pushed against the thread to look down at her legs. She saw the smattering of scratches from her first attempt the night before at shaving the fine, blonde hairs that grew there. Her toenails were painted a chipped coral and the polish shined in the fluorescence when one of the men clipped the braided friendship bracelet from her ankle.

Another of the men leaned over her left shoulder and slid a scalpel directly down her middle, slicing through the net and dividing her perfectly in half. Aphrodite's father stood behind a two-way mirror to the operating theater and watched the good men work. The procedure was his idea, a last desperate attempt to remember who his daughter was.

He began to notice early in the summer that things were changing. His friends acted differently around her. They no longer pulled her onto their laps to sit after dinner and listen to stories, opting instead to leave before the drinks were poured. Their wives hid glares under oversized sunglasses as the men kept their distance at the beach, eyes unfocused and necks taut as they scanned the sky directly above her head.

He, too, found himself growing uncomfortable around her when she came down for breakfast in pajamas, polka dot boxer shorts and a tank top, long hair piled sleepily atop her head. He strained to smile when he passed her the milk for her cereal and thought to himself, *If only her mother were here.*

After enduring months of this, he called in the experts for help. A single phone call was all it took to make the necessary arrangements and receive assurances that he would have his little girl back in no time. The procedure wouldn't be painful, they promised, no matter how it looked to the untrained eye. The girl wouldn't feel a thing and it really was best for everyone that they do it now while she was still small and quick to heal.

Two tray tables sat to the left of the patient with a culinary scale between them. The men pulled piece after bloody piece from her, weighed it, and placed it on one tray or the other.

They ripped from her the love of running through the woods, picking flowers, fairytales and fireflies, cuddling on the couch with her father over cups of hot chocolate. These were weighed and placed carefully on the first tray to be returned to her. "Heavenly," the men muttered in unison. "Heavenly." They added to the growing pile her piano lessons, her mother's banana bread recipe, and the prayers she whispered beside her bed on bent knees, each untinged with wantonness.

Then, they sliced away the butterflies in her stomach that took flight when she imagined the boy from sleepaway camp, his brown hair curling at the ends and nose freckled from the sun; the watermelon lip gloss roller that promised kisses in her future and made her lips taste like summertime. These were quickly cast aside. They then slid the blade in a lowercase "W" across the two halves of her chest, peeled away the growing flesh there, and threw it on the second tray with the bugs. "Common."

Aphrodite floated above the holy sterile field while the surgeons continued cutting and looked down at the two trays overflowing with all she was. A perfect division of heaven and earth.

Their work complete, the men bound a brand-new Aphrodite and returned her to her father, cotton stuffed between her legs. They explained to him how to change her bandages and ensure she healed without the world's infections.

Aphrodite's father beamed at his little girl and gathered her in a strong hug. Despite the pulses of pain, she smiled up at him and returned the embrace.

Homemaking in Wartime

We have watched our mothers, grandmothers, sisters, aunts and cousins work their fingers to the bone, blood seeping through the cracks in their cuticles and nails peeling like the dry skin of an onion, as they lay brick and mortar and floorboard to build their homes.

They weave carpets to pad the patter of tiny feet and shape dough into loaves to fill empty bellies. They smile as they crack open their sternums and expose the ventricles of their hearts, chambers turning to warm bedrooms where loved ones will sleep. They wind string lights through their ribs and share stories and proverbs amid the twinkling.

These homes are meant to be wrapped around cold shoulders and tucked under knees to keep out drafts. They are hugs with joists and studs that offer stability and a place to press your palm and feel the pulse of it all.

Some of us have been fortunate enough to raise our roofs in the lots adjacent to the heart homes of loving and kindred spirits. They have sustained us through lengthy phone calls and cups of coffee forgotten on end tables as we sort through the thousand casual cruelties that come with womanhood. Our property lines are a tangled mess of tender tangents, a patchwork quilt under which we huddle during the coldest of nights. It is a wonderful thing when individual toil can add to the communal village that we all know it takes to raise yourself, much less a child.

There is beauty, too, when one finds a way to be her own village. She lays down a floor mat with the design of a sprawling city; post offices and markets, movie theaters and dental offices, arranged around flat gray roads wide enough for Matchbox cars. She leans to smooth the surface of this mini metropolis and her son covers it in Fisher Price Little People, crayon drawn pine trees cut from cardboard, and plastic pizza savers repurposed into tiny tables to accommodate the residents' packed lunches. She voices the members of this created community and her son feels surrounded by loved ones. Yes, it takes a village to raise a child, and she conjures one right there on the living room floor.

And if she doesn't have a child living in the canyons of her chest, she does much the same. She scrapes out a patch of land for herself in the world and opens her heart for those to come. For these women, there often isn't a neighbor for miles and her own hearth must contain multitudes. In the quiet hours of the night, she chops carrots and potatoes and pieces of herself, propagating a support system of her own creation in glass jars placed on the kitchen windowsill. As the sunlight streams in, her roots grow deeper, and verdant leaves unfurl into a self-sustaining ecosystem. There is a strength in her solitary survival. And there is hope.

These villages, both large and small, are a marvel to behold. But open doors and open hearts sometimes let in more than we intend. Hidden behind loving words, sly smiles, and searching hands lie pillagers bent on conquering. Their sails drawn down to cloak their approach, they catch us off guard, hitting hard and fast before reinforcements can arrive.

Even in innocent exploration, they leave behind casualties of their curiosity. These Trojan Horse houseguests sample the lives of those inside, stretching and tearing as they try to force them to fit. They clean out stores of love and food alike, leaving us to starve. Carefully knit sanctuaries begin to fray at the edges and often nothing is left but ash and thread when the invaders cast them off and sail for new shores. Looting can look a lot like love.

Reconstruction after war can lead to a heart locked behind an iron gate. We aim to make something stronger and sturdier that won't leave us so exposed. In turn, the bulwark keeps out the good and bad alike, and a once happy home becomes a fortress. After such betrayal it seems only natural to bolt the doors and bar the windows. But that old inclination to welcome and host and hold is a hard habit to break.

Sometimes, all it takes is a single unexpected overnight guest to knock at the door. To settle down at your side, help spread the sorrow across the dining room table, and gather wood for the fireplace. They prompt us to bring blankets back out of cedar chests and remember. An understanding ear can cause hinges and latches to crumble, revealing rooms that we thought lost in the carnage.

In their reopening, the hearts that we build and rebuild turn tearful eyes out of windows to those living next-door. We pass brooms and dustpans in circles, sweeping pain through entryways and rehanging photographs in their broken frames. Potluck dinners and mimosa mornings pry open gates and expand borders. The fortress may fall when embraced by its neighbors, but your guest beds were never meant to stay made.

Stone & Honey

I loved the way you loved me, tender and removed. The smooth pieces of me that you claimed, rearranged, and presented to me in praises looked like a girl I used to know.

I loved that honey girl shining in your eyes. Reduced, refined, and familiar. I knew I could rest there for a while.

I loved the way you loved me as you led me by the hand through the shallows of my soul. Stopping to sit on the shoreline, you fell asleep fully clothed with your boots still on before the tide came in.

By your side, I dared not cast my eyes upon my own reflection; lest the terrible, writhing monster I'd become turn me to stone. I peeked at the creature from the safety of that beach, through the mirrors of your glasses as the eels swam circles at my feet. They curled around the jagged edges left over after I carved myself from clay, chisel still gripped in my fingers.

The ribs I formed by hand looked to you like your own.

I loved the way you loved me as you passed my power back to me in kind words and kisses. But in your gradual generosity, the gorgon grew hungry. The coiled vipers of my canyons rose to claim what was never yours to give. You offered my self back to me and I received my glory as a gift, crediting you for the life-giving light of my own sun.

But they refused. And in their taking, light found light. Your river rock nymph glimpsed her likeness in the sea while you slept, serpents still locked around her ankles. Her eyes sought out shining sharp corners and happily found them.

What you so kindly returned to me once you were finished writing my story fused to its host like socket and bone. The sound of my divine reconstruction drowned out your drowsy-sweet nothings like a single shout into the cave.

Like found like and gone was the fear of being turned to stone. Returned was the dangerous knowledge that I am of the stone. I created the stone. I molded the stone.

The masonry of stone on stone and light on self-illuminating light built my gaze and raised me above the crest of your eye line, revealing to me as you slept all that I forgot how to see.

Reflections

Oh, how I long to look upon myself as I once did, with soft eyes that are fully mine. To shed their scales that have grown brittle with exposure.

To again be led by the murmuring sound of cave waters that spread into a liquid plain and promise absolute acceptance.

I don't know when I first began to distinguish between water and sky and self, but that undifferentiated world feels lost to me.

It has been years since I laid down on that green bank and found a gleaming, watery shape that peered lovingly back at me. This crystalline likeness never questioned her place in the family of things, nor mine. She moved with the ripples and twinkled in the sunlight, owning them as parts of herself. But rather than hold onto her innate belonging, I left that familiar figure behind.

Despite the kind looks that shone up from the water, what else could I do but stand and follow straight where she could not go?

I was invisibly led to a world where I saw myself through the gaze of another who was less fair, less mild than my reflection. This intended individual solace of fellowship stripped me of the autonomy that led me to the lake in the first place.

Through these new eyes, looking upon myself with love feels like vain desire. My pool of pleasure has turned to salt tears. When I find myself out and bathing now, it is not that smiling mirror-image that my eyes seek out for reassurance.

They are instead cast up and around, scanning for other eyes on me.

They are cast inward, reminding me to pull my belly closer to my spine and sit straight to prevent it from folding.

They are cast down at my feet should I begin to enjoy the attention too much, forgetting my humility.

I can no longer see myself in innocence.

I am under the constant assault of awareness that the shape is my own. I ripped it from the surrounding context of connection and outlined its borders in a violent red.

I feel the amount of space it takes up in the world and long to shrink it down to something more manageable.

I search it for wrinkles and silver hairs, any reflective surface weaponized.

I blame it for not fitting into clothes that are too small to contain its supple wonder.

I punish it like a disobedient child with missed meals and cruel words that cut to the bone.

The bare skin that sparkled turned indecent upon further examination. The laughter that echoed from the shores sounds hollow and wholly too loud.

I am assured that I will live a long life, provided that I don't discover myself. Should I stay too long at the water's edge, I am likely to grow frail and consumed with my own image. But lately, the divine voice that first broke my silent self-contemplation has begun to grate like grinding teeth.

The repetition of its constant criticisms and reminders to pose for invisible cameras no longer hold my attention as they once did. My mind wanders from them, and I find myself drawn to more interesting topics of conversation.

So too am I often caught unawares by the sudden appearance of something that vaguely resembles the face I found in the water so many years ago. Despite the empty echoes of encircling hands that aim to drown her out, she appears peripherally.

I have seen her smiling in shop windows as I stroll through the city with my sisters.

She peers out at me through the wide eyes of my daughter that look up to me as we read books in bed.

I hear the lapping of her waves in laughter that sometimes escapes from me unbridled.

She whispers gentle reminders of the magic of our shared shape, of its elegant endurance.

As I bend to look, she bends just opposite. Still, I start back from her and she from me. Time has made us nearly strangers.

But should I return, pleased, she will be waiting with answering looks of sympathy and love, waiting with forgiveness and the cool caress of cave water.

Picking Flowers

There, in my circle of grass by the water's edge, knees pressed into the damp earth, spring felt eternal. Bees waltzed with flower buds and birds shared songs whose notes fell to me like raindrops from treetops. The blossoms that blended in my basket held infinite possibilities.

When my work was complete, I could weave crowns of daisies or dry dandelions to brew tea.

I could bunch them into bouquets, bring them with bread and honey to adorn the tables of those I love as we shared a meal.

I could scatter their seeds across a small plot of land, grow the roots of a home of my own somewhere and settle down.

The smell of the narcissus's tepals, fully formed inside the bulb long before we met in the meadow, promised peace. Mixing its crown with spirits, I could craft a balm for my mother's worries. On the mornings that she can't summon the strength to wake, I could press the perfume into the papery thin skin of her wrist. Moving my fingers in slow circles, I could help it seep into the blue streams that crisscross there, the same waterways that flow through me. She could ride the slow current of our blood bond out of her bed and into the world without fear.

***

The daffodil's trumpet heralded your arrival before the ground had time to split. I reached for its trembling head, my heart's only desire to somehow still its shivering. In my urgency, the basket toppled over, and an entire day's labor was lost.

I saw each of my individual futures float with the flowers above the abyss as though suspended. Unsure of which to save, I spared not one from that hungry mouth. My first sight of you like some great god of the underworld left me frozen, hand stuck clutching the single daffodil.

I can't be sure of the flowers' fates, but they were lost to me. Asters, lilies, and hyacinths in every hue gone. Rather than let them burn to ash or think to raise them to rest on the lake's surface, I think it more likely that you took each of my beloved blossoms in lieu of blood; you could not be denied your offering at the entry gates.

You took me as an offering, too. Plucked me from my field like any other. The dark waves of your love swallowed me whole and I thought I could drown. Stomach dropping, I reached for your hand before I could bring myself to meet your eyes.

And despite all that I left behind in the meadow, I grew to like the way your thumb laid flat against my knuckles.

***

You pressed it hard in laughter when we raced down long hallways, the sound of bare feet slapping against the walls.

You slid it across my palm, sending shivers down my spine as you read our future in its lines.

You moved it slowly in my same imagined circles along the papery thin skin of my hand, my worries lifting with every rotation.

But these grounding moments didn't last. With no great dog or three judges to decide my place in your world, I looked to you for guidance. I clung to you in our marriage bed. I searched your eyes as they stared into mine, trying to find any trace of the desperate need that led you to take me.

In your haste, you forgot that a love must be watered and fed, if it is to have any chance at survival. You placed me with the rest of your collection—one of many pretty things—and, satisfied, left me to starve on scraps and seeds.

I pressed my own thumb to the ridges of my fingers and learned to breathe through my hunger for you. I let stomach pangs devour nervous butterflies and bit my tongue to a bloody pomegranate pulp to stop myself from begging you to stay.

In your distance, you made me a shallow grave of a girl; my eternal spring replaced with a field of mourning. I buried my fresh-faced feelings alive without looking. I laid them down deep below the rows of flowers in my chest with the worms and the maggots to decay.

***

I slept in the shadows of myrtle groves so long that the sun could barely reach me. In the end, it was my mother who brought the light to me there. She led me by the hand from my loneliness. She brushed the grass from my hair, washed the mud off my face, and held me like a child.

After that bright equinox, my mouth watered at the thought of filling myself with all I had been denied. She baked loaves of fresh bread and we spread warm slices with butter and jam. I showered and slept in her feather bed. Again, I dreamed of bountiful bouquets. But your seeds took hold the moment they passed from fingers to lips and left no room for another love.

***

I woke to feel them growing deep within my guts. I left my mother's home while she slept and walked back to my old familiar field, basket in hand. But I was no longer welcome there. I watched as the wildflowers, one by one, wilted before my eyes. There wasn't a single one fit for picking. Your roots snaked through my insides, stretching and ripping and weighing me down. They pulled until my bones buckled and I was pinned to the meadow.

I bowed before my fate eternal, knees pressed into the cold and unforgiving dirt between us. I had no choice but to drag myself back to you. I scraped at the earth, fingernails falling like petals as I searched. Laid beneath a display of bright yellow daffodils, the undead longing for you rose from its grave and stood to face me. Beetles scurried through vacant eye sockets that somehow softened. It held my bloody hand in its own. The exposed, boney tip of a thumb snaked around my fingers and laid flat. Its cold touch kept me company as we sat and waited at your empty table.

Dear Odysseus,

It's been lonely loving you. I've written too many of these letters. Ever the prudent and constant wife, I turned to them as one should a journal or a friend. Without my own crew of companionable sailors, I've laid bare for you the tedium that is life alone.

I told you of plaiting my hair and washing my face in cold water to begin each day anew. I shared the strange dreams that swirl through my head as I sleep—flashes of eagle talons ripping through downy gooseflesh; four springs in a row, bubbling clear and cold; an eternal maiden, her lovely braids wrapping like rope around your wrists—and the cold sweat that follows them. I wrote these things, put them in a drawer, and tried not to hold them close.

My hands are growing mangled and tight-fisted from my grip on the pen, something I once thought romantic when I imagined yours feeling much the same clasped around the halyard. I hoped that, one day, these papers would be our kindling. We would strike a match, hold it to their corners, and watch as our time apart went up in dark swirls of smoke. Warmed by the fire, our fingers, stiffened in solitude, would slacken. We would pry open our hearts and hands and heal together. And while it's true that I never sent these bottled messages, you never wrote me back.

It seems decades now that you've been gone. I can't count the days anymore or I think I'd go mad. When you left, it was to fight monsters. You conjured these beasts that simply couldn't be abided. You told me you were doing this for me, for us; that you had a cause. I thought it was noble, I really did. I scooped out my heart when you left and packed it with your things, raw and pulsing with hope. I trusted that it would be precious cargo on your ship, a beacon back home to me.

But now, I find myself too often casting reality aside in favor of writing. Slumped over this damned desk, every night I pick up my pen. I turn it from the page and dig its sharp point into that hollow place that you left in me. I stab and twist until I can feel something that resembles my old heart beating. The cave in my chest has grown and deepened to join the pit in my stomach. My emptiness sloshes with ink and bile. I fear that one of these nights I may fall in and never escape.

So many years ago, you told me that there was no finer, greater gift than the life we shared. That a man and a woman could possess their home, that their minds and hearts could work as one. Maybe once that was true of us, but it hasn't been for some time. You left our home exposed, forcing me to build a bulwark, bolt the doors and bar the windows. You left me to a life of solitary confinement.

I'm no fool, Odysseus. I hear rumors of what goes on out there. The lips and tongues you've tasted while I waited for you. The nymphs with the lovely braids. And no matter how fully I shut myself up in here, the fog of knowing finds me. It seeps through beneath the door, creeps up my form, and rolls over my mouth and nose. It smothers me as I sleep alone in our bed.

The figure I've conjured up in my mind is wasting away. I can see his spectral ribs. His uncanny smile, it's not quite right. If I close my eyes in a rare moment of silence and focus with all that's in me, I can almost weave the crinkles around your eyes. The fleshy earlobes are nearly there. The fine hairs of your forearms come so close to being caught in the wind. I breathe deeply and imagine that it's you I inhale. But the air is thin up here.

I held fast for as long as I could. As scores of suitors beat down our door and demanded that I renounce my ties to you, I wove patience into my hopes for your return only to have them unravel in my hands each night before the sun rose. I've delayed and diverted, waiting for you to send it all away. But I can no longer sit idle as I have.

Among the mysteries that made their way back to me were whispers of creatures who live on a flowery island out at sea. These honey-voiced monsters are described by some as slick, scaled things that slither through the cracks in the rocky shore. Others say they are covered in a thick down of oily feathers. Still, one detail remains through each telling: they have great power. It was my plan to beg them to change me.

If I could become one of these Aegeanfish-tailed maidens, I could swim to you and stay your course. I imagined you seeing my form rise from the waters and your stoic face melting into tears. I thought that I would leave this life behind, gladly. I would join you out there on the seas of red wine that you love so much. Their pull would start to make sense to me, and I could see how it was so easy for you to turn your back on all that we had for just a chance to conquer those demons. And even if you didn't know I was there, I would mast along with you and somehow you would feel less alone. And yet...

After securing passage to their isle, it was no small feat to make my way to them. The captain of my ship would not venture close. Unsure of the welcome I would receive from these murderous beasts, I swallowed my fear like a pill, shed my gown before the captain's hungry eyes, and dove into the waves. The current there, as you well know, rips and tears. I was bruised and bloodied by the time I washed up onto their shore.

With an unexpected tenderness, they applied a salty balm to my fair skin and wrapped it in seaweed for protection from the midday sun. I slept beside my new companions for several days before my strength returned. When I woke, it was to an apple-faced girl whose long hair trailed across my face as she tended my wounds. Her hands held a gentle strength; her mouth, a strawberry pink pout. It was her face that flooded my new dreams and the longing to see it anew that pulled me from my bed.

Each night, we gathered around a fire. As she and her sisters sang to me their ancient melodies, I taught them to weave fibers into nets to gather fish. Time on the island moved slow and sweet as poured molasses. Sure, there were ships that sailed too close, but the fault lay with them alone. We cannot be blamed for their taking our intimate exchanges as invitations. And we were so hungry.

My new home is not unfamiliar to you. I was told that when you passed its coast, you filled your men's ears with wax and stole the sirens' secrets for yourself alone. That sounds like you. But me, I had no one left to melt down Circe's gifts and remind me what it was my compass pointed towards. So, I stayed. And I listened. And I begged.

My request was a simple one, they said. And their magic that promised gills to ride the waves to you were tempting at first. But I took too quickly to swimming and singing and sisterhood. Now, I think a home with them on the shore sounds restful. I've misplaced that old need to follow your ship like an albatross. And with it, I lost my fear of the crossbow's bite.

There's more I could share with you, but I fear I must rest my pen now. The sutures that fastened my legs ache with the sirens' stitching and the gashes along my neck are still fresh from the razor's edge. They stuffed my empty ribcage with music and mead, and I am unaccustomed to such fullness.

I will try to send these pages in a bottle tossed off the cliff, but I cannot guarantee they will reach you. I'm unsure to whom I am writing, whom I should address on the glass. You once said your name was "Nobody." Was it loneliness that led you to say that? I can no longer remember. And I can no longer relate.

Fondly,
Penelope

Salt

Remember the wife of Lot.

As though I could forget her.

Remember the wife of Lot.

As though I was not her in some past life.

Remember the wife of Lot.

As though I am not her in this very life.

This woman, unnamed and unknown but for her quiet rebellion, lives deep and disobedient within me like a nesting doll. Her great sin, if you've forgotten, was daring to look back at all she left behind. She was meant to steel her breaking heart to the destruction of her home. To walk away without hesitation. Without hurt.

As though she had ever known anything but this city swept away.

As though she wasn't ripping herself raw from the fly paper, leaving half behind.

As though she lost all right to the bits and pieces living on in a now-gone world.

As though the pull of the past is an easy thing to shrug off.

Archangel and hellfire breathing down her neck, she failed to follow this singular command. In the face of a similar eternity, Orpheus failed as well. In their good company, I, too, have failed.

I have scattered myself across continents, only to pause and move back through time to mourn each late life as I would a child.

Without divine intervention, it can take years to build a pillar of salt.

Whoever tries to keep their life will lose it, and whoever loses their life will preserve it. It's all the same to me.

My holy temple split in two. I tried to hold it together, gripping cut stone as fingers bent and broke. I held fast until shoulders sprang from sockets. Reluctantly, I unclenched my fists and left its pieces as an offering to the past.

I tried to remember Lot's wife.

I tried to forget how it felt to be yours.

My in-sincerest apologies to the angry archangel. I have left the housetop and gone down to retrieve myself from the rubble. Burning sulfur rains down around me and I feel myself go salty.

I look back at a beach in the Carolinas and count out a collection of shells before my hand brushes yours.

I am the salt of sea spray on sunburnt summer skin.

I look back at a meadow in Germany and lay a blanket by the pond where we'll rest until life leads us home again.

I am the salt of a picnic basket pretzel, soft and shared.

I look back at a rooftop in Naples and trace the tangle of limbs beneath a sky stuffed with stars before we knew how deep love could grow.

I am the salt of slate tiles slick with sweat.

I look back at our first dance together and listen as, heads thrown back in raucous laughter, we claim it as the first day of our life.

I am the salt of falling tears on our faces.

I look back at the birth of our daughter, two turned one turned three, and scream her into being, certain that it is the first day of my life.

I am again the salt of falling tears on our faces.

I look back at our last night together, shoulders slumped as we cut one life into two, and slam the door on your cries that this is the last day of your life.

I am always the salt of falling tears on our faces.

Without divine intervention, it can take years to build a pillar of salt.

Remember the wives of Lot.

Taming

For every bull who has flattened a village, whose heavy hooves level houses without hesitation, there is a girl who could bow, press her head to the ground and with barely a thought, stop his stride. There is much she could do, and much she has done, on this earth that she makes into heaven.

Her quiet voice could carry to ask his name and end his path of destruction.

Her nimble fingers could bend to bolster the blossoms and bind the branches he's broken.

Her fluid feet could lead, taking slow, tilling steps that leave the land unblemished.

Her strong hands could plant patience that grows in garden rows and harvest a heart that is open.

You see, befriending mere beasts is no great feat for she who has made Hell her home. With her green thumbs, she could knead and she could rub, and mold a man from the mass of a monster. There is much she could do, and much she has done, on this earth that she makes into heaven.

She could share with him the girlish secret of silently swallowing screams.

She could teach the art of turning cold cheeks and the constraint that binds her wings.

She could reveal her rage locked in its cage and explain how it never escapes.

She could beg and she could plead, and she could want and she could need, and she could even call it fate.

Once she's planted and plowed, once she's weeded and wept, she could climb upon his back. Through the spring they could run, and the war would be won, the world all the safer for it. There is much you can do, and much you have done, on this earth that you make into heaven.

But this bull that you love loves wrestling doves and it isn't your duty to stop him. Cast your eyes to the past, how it lingers and lasts, and remember the dangers you face. Just as Titan shoulders splinter, maiden backs may be broken by the weight of a fragile man.

So let him tend his own garden, let your heart slightly harden, and let the sky learn to carry its own weight.

An Apology to the Muses

What place is there for consent in the life of a muse? Is agreement assumed from the first spark of inspiration? Is her life a series of mutual exchanges of ideas and beauty, or simple theft? Theft of time, theft of moments and memories.

Does she whisper her stories under drawn covers and by candlelight, offering them up as sacrifices to be made immortal? Does she seek her face in frescoes and wait for the day when a song is finally called by her name? Or does she just hope for connection, one strong enough to drown out her beloved's constant cacophony of creation? I don't know.

It seems a waste for all muses to go the way of Calliope; holding scrolls they surely would have written themselves had they been given the voice. It is hard not to wonder where you found yours. We didn't spend time speaking of who taught you to think the way you do. I don't know if there was some grand tutor, some man or woman of twists and turns, who came into your life before I did. Maybe there was. Maybe you soaked up all that they had to say, passing their wisdom on to me over candlelight and the smoke of your smudging sage. But I think the brilliance was probably you all along.

I've written you countless dedications, love letters penned under the flood of streetlights begging you to come back. I've put our story on paper, balled it up, and dropped it in the bin as the ink ran from the page, words blending with the takeout containers and napkins scrawled with your favorite lines by Cummings. I promised you that anything cast into the net of these writings will be spared the trash heap, so I send you this: one last hope that you'll see. That you'll know. That the tender comprehension will return once more. That this isn't yet another taking.

Let this be my first draft attempt at reciprocity. At restitution. A message in a bottle filled with reminders of the night we spiked our drinks, and the majority of this book came pouring out as I shouted into the void that was your lover, sitting across the couch from me, his pupils as large as the moon that held your gaze for hours?

Even then, when this all began, I felt your distance. I felt your ebbs and flows as you tried to chart the course of what it was we were doing. I felt the tide pull us under as the ice cream dripped down our chins and the street preacher howled in the backdrop of our perfect day.

You held my hair back as I retched out the bile in me that coalesced on these pages, and you plastered my heart so the cracks could fuse. Together, we made something intangible and fleeting. It was a wonder, this thing that sprouted under the shine of your sunlight and the eternal spring of my sadness.

And still, I saw it as I do all perfect things in life: as plot. I've lived a thousand stories. Tragedies, comedies, coming of age after coming of age. All of them, I laid bare for you, and you offered me yours in return. We spent afternoons in quiet bookshops, running our fingertips up and down the spines of Garcia Marquez, Murakami, and Plath, entwining our own memoirs among the likes of Walls and Karr. Each just another story for the other to drink in.

You told me once that we spoke in poetry and felt in film, and I think you were right. I listened as you told me of the peach and the fountain, and the meaning of it all. But while you opened your heart to feed our creation, the heavy doors to my study closed behind my eyes as I nodded along to all that you said. I swept you off your feet by the ankles and shook until there was nothing left landing on the ground for me to gather.

I don't know, now, if you've forgotten the slants of sunlight through the window blinds, the way they painted you in stripes that swirled with smoke. I don't know if that green and brown painting, with its sloping lines inspired by shared secrets and a glass of champagne, still hangs in your bathroom. I don't know if you've found a way to fill the emptiness that my starving left behind in you.

But I do know this: there is a certain taking that comes with inspiration. There is a selfishness, too. I still pray to you when I pray at all; and for that, I'm sorry.

Fragments

Unlike her talkative sisters, the tenth muse reveals herself to us in pieces.

Pieces of papyrus.

Parchment scraps.

Pottery shards.

And poem fragments.

Scant offerings scattered across the ancient world and dragged, kicking and screaming, into modernity.

These are the unlikely places where we find her hiding. She refuses to appear to us in dreams and ignores our prayers. Our desperate need for that small, still and resounding voice is none of her concern. But despite her avoidance, we dig and we grasp and we pry her words from antiquity.

We presume to understand the whole of her wisdom.

We force fusion on what remains and attempt to reassemble the spectral voice.

We latch on to her meager offerings of mangled verse and give in to the temptation to complete her thoughts.

We assign to them great meaning; unknown context be damned.

But each newly discovered turn of phrase, each flawed attempt at timely translation, only serves to further obscure her image.

I have known this fragmentary woman, so much as such a woman can be known. And so often have I found myself seized by an unbearable longing to put to words this knowing, and its companion of wanting, which she doled out in equal measure.

If I could but take all that she left behind and sculpt the slivers to form an idyll in her name, I know that I could cure this sickness and soothe this grief. Surely, once my pen kissed page I would recall the love once tasted. It should come easily because, as I am called to remind both reader and writer alike, I have known her.

I have lain by her side, spring rain making music through the screen of a bedroom window while we savored the sweetness of Venus.

I have seen how her eyes match and mirror the water of a koi pond in the afternoon sunlight; how her face glows golden as she smiles down at a sunflower.

I have felt the skin of her cheek: smooth, supple, and speckled, beneath my fingertips as we stopped to stand on a street corner.

I have tasted the peppermint that lingered on her lips as we leaned close over cups of tea long grown cold.

I have happily swallowed the venom, irresistible and bittersweet. Loose-limbed and loose-lipped, I have gladly let a reptilian love strike me down.

I have glimpsed our afterlife, collective ashes eternally entombed, entangled, and indistinguishable in a single golden urn.

I have burned with the need to drag my fingernails through bloody flesh, to crack bones; to hold her rabbit's heart in my hand. To excavate, expose, examine, and own it.

But mine was not the wild hyacinth that lay unguarded in a field, torn and trodden underfoot. She is made of sturdier stuff.

She possessed no slender stem with which I could pluck her from her peace.

As yet unbroken, she was the poet's other: that joyous apple, reddening and removed. Should any fool caught in the sticky web of desire stretch to reach for her bough, she is bound to retreat to her castle in the clouds. She will leave their despairing hands to close on nothing but empty air.

I have known her, and so too have I known the mad passion that possessed Daphnis to defile his orchard's only offering.

I have felt the rush of wind between knuckles and registered the void. I have come to understand how, upon seeing just one remaining apple high in the tree, he could not abide its being there any longer.

He was consumed with fear that it may fall to rot, be flattened beneath trampling hooves, or worse yet: remain untouched as something whose perfection was only to be admired from afar. What could he do then, but rip the fruit from its host and lay claim to its majesty? I have known the fear that made him commit this crime.

I have been brought to near madness at the sight of sunlight slanting between barren branches.

I have felt the salty sting of near death by a thousand cuts, each attempt to close the stubborn space slicing slightly deeper.

I have allowed my lonely arms to reach, as fated to fail as they were cursed to commit.

But, unlike that brutal beau, I know all too well the fierce desire towards protection that drove desperation into his lover's cries.

I have starved beside my Sappho, begging our backyard garden to bear fruit. There's a word for when broccoli turns from food to flower: bolting. If the soil is too dry or wet, the air too hot or cold, the bed too crowded or sparse; the plant will set to flower and take its leave. It will no longer sustain its master. Apples are much the same.

Chloe was intimately acquainted with the truths that lie in both apples and taking, as all women are. She fought to protect the fruit's defining distance. When Daphnis knelt to lay it at her feet, plucked and pruning, as an offering to her aphroditic beauty, the heart he sought to win broke at the seizure of that which could never be again.

The poet imagined achieving immortality, an eternal revenant of writing that would be remembered and inherited by all those yet to come. Would she smile to learn that her pervasiveness bred permanence? Would she care that it was all she didn't share that has left us longing for more? Like the apple she so dutifully described, she avoids our every advance and leads us in a dance through time.

Lucky Sappho, to live on in a world where we so often find imagination at the core of desire. And lucky us, to get to follow such graceful steps.

The Cicada & the Dawn

It is a great endeavor each morning to pull myself from our bed. The lingering warmth and weight of your arm across my ribs beckon me to stay. The satin sheets entangling our legs pull me down like the Kraken. But I must break these ties and take to my work. Again, again.

In the last of the moonlight, I step silently out onto our shore and make way for that fraternal sun to bring a new day. Casting my eyes to the heavens, I see what I have been dreading most. The moon's halo and thin wisps of clouds warn of the snow to come. With it, you are bound to take your leave. Our bed is doomed to grow cold with the season. The sun's reign will shorten, and I will soon forget what it was to have you there. I cannot stop the snow, no matter how bright the new day's sun may be. There is but one path to retention and I see it clearly.

As the morning light spreads, I make my way to Zeus. On my knees, with eyes wet, I beg—knowing that if the snow has time to reach you, you will be pulled from me should he refuse to intervene. A small mercy, he bows his head and answers my prayer.

Heading home to you, I watch the sun lift the veil of snow clouds and pray that you haven't woken in time to see them. I find you just as you were, nestled below the plush, downy layers we laid together. I put to the shining doors and go to you. We start the day as the one before, time folding in on itself until it is only the moon's morning dance with the sun that reminds me of its passing. Each time I wake before you and see the clouds beginning to thin, I beg Helios to burn them away; to keep you there with me, wrapped in my arms of flowers. The loyal star holds back the winter, and we stay.

But one morning, our temporal mirror cracks when I see the silver spreading across the crown of your head. Your face is pinched in sleep. Between your eyebrows, a new crevice has deepened and your hold around my chest is slack. It's too easy to cleave myself from you and I know. I rise from our bed, and you turn from me, exhaling as though in relief.

That night, we pass a bottle between us, and you smile softly as you look over my shoulder for the frost. The misery in your eyes calls for mercy. Once I hear your deep sighs of coming sleep, I give you the last gift that I can.

I watch as your wide shoulders shrink and your head curls forward. Your numerous legs, pitifully thin, wave helplessly before my eyes. I bend to carefully scoop you up and the length of you can now fit in the palm of my hand. In your new form, you can go beneath ground when the air turns crisp and emerge when the dawn is its brightest.

In your times of rest, you are free of monotony's endless babbles, still and waiting for me. Throughout these cold days, I leave the home that we share. I roam and drink in the shimmer of snow on mountaintops. I let the clouds turn to mist and the moon's ring shine down on me as you wait, buried in the hard layers of dirt that I laid alone. I see fields painted white and watch as winter streams flow beneath the spreading ice of their surface. I store up bits of momentary magic, letting them bring me to you.

Soon, the night grows warmer, and it is not such a struggle to welcome the dawn. The earth opens and you make your way back to me, screaming and desperate. Hearing your cries, I cannot bring myself to tell you of all that you've missed. Instead, I hold it in my heart as I hold you in my hand for another season.

***

Is this our fate, then? To cling to something fleeting and lose the rhythm of change that made our time so precious? No. No, it can't be.

If it is my curse from Aphrodite to love that which can never stay, I will sing her praises for showing me the perfection in finitude. Better that Artemis's gentle arrow strike you dead than I strip you of the flow of the life that you have lived so rapturously.

I won't let your deep woods decay and fall, nor the vapors of confinement weep their burden into the contours of your wide chest. I won't trap you in my jar of a heart with bones and stones and bits of cloth, nor place you on an altar as an offering. Though Zeus would surely grant my wish and stop the sliding sands of our hourglass, it is the knowledge of love that makes us immortal.

So, I put this terrible dream out of my mind. I bring the dawn again to the world, and to you. I let my steps lead me home and away from that tempting torture, with good news that your time has come. With rosy fingers, I help as you gather up your things and watch you arm yourself in plush layers that you lay without me. Your feet fall silently with the snow, you recede, and the settling flakes fill in the spaces where you once were.

Standing at the crest of our dunes, you smiled as you told me of the beauty in true Wilderness; how these unlikely peaks of Oceanus retain their power and wonder through their absolute refusal to be tamed. As the wind imposes its force on them, the saltation of each individual grain moves and shapes the whole and no permanence is permitted. They are a fluid thing and our snapshots of them are fleeting. I responded that, for me, much of their magic was in held the improbability that I got to share them with you. But, of course, we were really describing the same thing.

So, I will look back fondly on this time when my knees were light to dance as fawns. And when the tears fall to form fresh dew on the grass, the droplets will sustain me through our times of drought. I will wrap myself in a watery cloak of memory.

Your clear, song loving lyre will play me back to myself and our truth.

When I close my eyes, I'll see the flicker of firelight that gleamed in yours as you played, and I won't groan for this or long for further gifts of you from the violet-capped Muses. On those cold and lonely mornings, I will smile up at the moon's halo. I'll see the clouds cupping the edges as the petals on a flower know that all is as it is meant to be.

To Carry a Mousa

It started with sketches. I spent days locked away, making a studio of my mind and pouring over charcoal smudges meant to capture the way light dances in your eyes. But the pages of my notebook were no match for my yearning. I gripped your likeness until paper crumbled in my hands, tears falling and turning you to pulp. The marble was much sturdier.

I chipped away at that block, heavy chunks crashing to the floor as I searched for you. I swung in wide arcs, lifting my rasp between each blow and brushing away your excess. Chest heaving, my heart's muscle memory and my hands' love labor brought you back to me. With each strike, the pointed chisel went deeper, unleashing you like a lily leaning towards spring.

The hammer and point found the slope of your nose, led me down the line of your jaw. They showed me the part of your lips, flesh like fruit I have held between biting teeth in communion. Your arms reached out to me once again and my legs quaked at the memory of your fingers' well-traveled roads.

Finally freed, I washed the translucent surface of your cold shape to smooth it. Pure and white as milk, I found you free of the ravages of time and faults of nature. I stood before you, my heart drinking the flames of a burning love, brighter even than the torches lighting your face of snowy ivory.

Each time I returned to my temple, it was as though you were caught motionless for but a moment. I would watch and wait for those full lips to curve into a smile, the almond eyes to crinkle and laughter to shake the walls. Always, you refused.

I laid bones and stones and bits of cloth at your feet. I placed flowers in your hair. I prayed to my false idol daily and imagined the things you'd say if stone could speak. I let my searching hands roam, certain the sculpture would soon soften. But I loved a lifeless thing.

Retreating further, I curled my body against the base of your pedestal and slept a restless sleep. My dreams were drenched in dove's blood.

Behind my closed eyes, the flames around you leapt three times and I woke with a start in our bed. Feeling my fear, you pulled me to you, pulse steady beneath warm skin that gave like wax in the sun. And my hands met a new medium.

Stitches

Standing in the shower, I run my hand down the slope of my side. Slick with soap, it slides so quickly over the stitches that I can almost believe I imagined them. My frantic fingers find the knot of one hidden below the teardrop of a breast, another poking out between two boney ribs.

Irregular and uneven, they're clearly a rush job. I press them flat, flesh rising to cover what the night exposed. With them, I push down the fear that my lover felt my unraveling ties beneath their fingers.

Fear that sutures scraped skin as we lay with legs entwined. Fear that tempted fingers reached for them as I slept. Fear of falling to pieces like the ribbon-necked bride of my childhood nightmares.

These bumps and tendrils seem to me an ugly, pitiful thing; the unfortunate result of a haphazard attempt at containment. It's hard to anticipate when they will make their presence known. Hands roaming across my body, the strands rise with my pulse. Clear-minded, I can will them to pull taut and keep my longing below the surface. But lost in the bliss of one too many caresses, they are wont to rise like gooseflesh. A lingering look, a single shared laugh, are enough to call forth the protrusions. The void beside me aches like a phantom limb.

I dread the thought of falling asleep in the comforting arms of another, only to wake and find myself threadbare from armpit to ankle. To find my loneliness so exposed. Left to wrap myself in top-sheets or too-big t-shirts; draw the curtains tight and hide from morning.

As I lather, rinse, and repeat, I consider getting it over with. Taking a seam ripper down my side, pulling them up one by one and violently undoing Apollo's repairs. I think I could embrace a temporary existence of exposure, of guts and gore, if it led me to a life that could be shared.

I'd bind my body tight in gauze each day and relish the luxurious release of spilling myself out over crisp, white sheets come nightfall. I'd make friends with the entrails that squirm and hunger inside of me. Make them dinner and ask them their favorite color. Find their fears, harness their hopes, and give them a bear hug. Maybe then I could give them some true company. The first cut would be as easy as breathing.

What I find hard to fathom is the process of rejoining this loosened self with another. Laid out beside my beloved, if they could bare their own insides, would connection be a seamless fusing? A painless return to Plato's two-faced, eight-limbed soulmate monsters of the past?

Or would my cells reject another's once they were known? Would we be forced to pass a new needle and thread between us, to pierce twin holes of devotion until we were nothing but scar tissue and string?

Turning off the shower, this fashioned creature of companionship, half made up, feels to me like an improvement upon my current patchwork self—but only slightly. I stand in the mirror and search myself for any loose ends. Confident I am concealed, I walk back into the bedroom.

My lover is laying on their side, snoring softly in the slanting light of my window blinds. It isn't hard to see myself tethered to them there, a mess of love and limbs. Hope swells as I scan their body for signs of needlework, a matching wound to meet mine. Yet again, I find nothing but unblemished, sun-soaked skin. And reach for my razor.

Γαλανός (Galanos)

There may be no truth to it, but I heard once that the ancient Greeks had no word for the color blue.

That Homer wrote of rolling waves of wine because a sanguine Shiraz came as close to capturing how the seas shimmer in sunlight as his language would allow.

It's probably bullshit, but I'd like to travel to them all the same.

I'd like to shove us in a big, blue suitcase and drag it back through time.

I'd seat myself on that old Grecian shoreline and tear the zippers from their seams.

I'd watch our lapis lazuli love turn to dust in the silence.

"Azure,

    Azure,

        Azure,"

You'd beg me again for a first, second, and final time, but it would be lost in translation.

Division & Surrender of Property Short Form*

This agreement is intended to be a final disposition of the matters addressed herein and may be used as evidence and incorporated into a binding, legal decree. Division of property has been determined as follows:

I, ___________________________, subsequently referred to as the Surrenderer, hereby relinquish all claim—past, present, and future—to the enclosed personal property on this, the __ day of ______, ______. The Surrenderer waives all rights and access to the aforementioned property. Once the enclosed is surrendered to and received by _________________________, subsequently referred to as the Respondent, it will not be returned.

      1. The Surrenderer retains all rights to and ownership of the following:

The holy hue of blue eyes soaked in moonlight, dark and deep as quicksand.

The feel of a hand coming to rest on a bare shoulder, light as a fallen leaf.

The terpene, equine smell inhaled, flashes of a thing strong and pulsing between legs in the forest.

The haven of being held in firm arms, chest tucked under chin, dancing slow as dripping honey.

The predictable path a thumb travels

to cheek,

      to clavicle,

         to coxal.

The anticipation of flesh on flesh, cloaked in the delicious delay of thin cotton and concentrated restraint.

And every moment before, when I didn't know you from Adam.

The Respondent assumes all rights to and ownership of the enclosed, inventoried here for reference:

The autumn air that swirled as I stood waiting for you in the courtyard.

The muffled sound of your steps through grass that floated over my shoulder.

The night sky's clear, cloudless contrast.

The constellations you asked me to name:

Ursa Major,

> *Orion,*

>> *Cygnus.*

The intimacy of lone, hushed voices in the dark.

The head of curls laid in a lap.

The crimson cupid's bow.

The way it curved around name and neck.

The arch of one body eager for another.

The hand cupping the fleshy place where thighs kiss.

The moment's turn towards hesitation from one side.

The next moment's turn towards violence from another.

The familiar rush of pine through nostrils.

The newly added note of sweat turned sour.

The bile that rose at the scent.

The bone-white line where lips once lived.

The impossibly long and looming collum.

The blue veins visible; thick, erect and aroused.

The blushing arms, pinned and spread like wings.

The desperate kicking and clawing.

The foregone futility in fighting back.

The terrified, vague and fumbling fingers.

The loss of familiarity and ownership

of fingers,

      of hands,

           of self.

The smothered scream silenced by a damp palm.

The sound of a skull cracking on concrete.

The spilling of blood.

The blurring of vision.

The taking and destruction

of choice,

    of innocence,

        of faith.

The launching of a thousand ships.

The burning of a homeland.

The refusal to intervene.

The rejection of empathy.

The rising red tide of hatred, both inside and out.

The insatiable glutton that is guilt.

The inheritance of that guilt by our daughters.

And the longing to be laid, white ash amid funereal cypresses.

______________________________ __________

Signature of Surrenderer   Date

______________________________ __________

Signature of Respondent   Date

**Originally published in the 21st edition of*
Oberon poetry magazine

Breakfast Thoughts

I spent the morning making oatmeal and considering the relationship between rage and wrath. How delicately they dance, steps so slow and seductive you start to sway along. There is obvious symmetry in the pairing. They are arguably perfect partners. Weightlessly, they waltz, bodies bound and buoyed by wired rhythms of tension and release. The former leads and the latter follows like a foregone conclusion; footloose, fancy-free, and fucking deadly.

I stirred in raisins and brown sugar, sweetening my breakfast to the brink of dessert. I don't much like oatmeal, but it gets the job done. Even when eaten alone, standing hunched over the kitchen sink conscious of crumbs, it sits in the stomach hearty and full of nutrients.

On other mornings much like this one, I have filled my bowl instead with rage. Unsweetened and free of wrinkled raisins; it was all bitterness and bite. I rolled it around on my tongue like a stone and sucked. I tucked it in the pocket of my cheek, stashed away for winter. But you can starve on rage alone.

I'd like to ask the gods to describe the taste of wrath.

My old Father God, did your mouth water in time with the clouds' 40 days of rain, your people drowning to the sound of your stomach growling thunderclaps through the sky?

Majestic Hera, did you chew the flesh of Lamia's children like cud after you led them from their mother, little lambs to the slaughter?

Mighty Zeus, did you first find yourself famished from the fight, then feasting alongside the eagle on endless cuts of liver roasted to perfection over an open fire that was yours all alone?

Did it taste sweet like brown sugar, exacting revenge and giving legs to your loathing?

You see, I haven't known such ravenous relief. For while they may bring about a beautiful ballet for a powerful few, rage and wrath rarely appear together these days. I have found the former to be curiously commonplace, buried in the bellies of women everywhere, while the latter is steeped in privilege and notably absent from supermarket shelves.

I have been denied even a bite of the just desserts for the countless crimes against my humanity. Sticks and stones have broken my bones and words have wounded my heart. But my offenders went unpunished, clever as they were to attack a mere mortal. A girl, even.

Sitting at the table and tallying up my grievances over a cup of coffee, I thought that perhaps I would mix my rage with wrath if given the chance. I would scoop and stir, blend and bake them into something best served cold. I would feel my too-tense-for-far-too-long tethers slacken in their partner's capable hands. Wire would fall away with every bite. Hell, maybe I would even dance alongside them once my legs broke free. But even then, when the music stopped, I would be eating alone, standing hunched over the kitchen sink conscious of crumbs.

So, I added a little more sugar to the bowl of oatmeal and left my remaining rage in the refrigerator to rot. I shoved it to the back by the bag of wilted baby spinach and shut the door.

They both taste like shit anyway.

Act One

Curtain opens on a blacked-out stage. The silhouette of a woman is visible center-stage, seated on a stool. An occupied choral riser is almost visible upstage. Backlit spotlight turns on and off at the mention of each name; though illuminated, the woman's face remains obscured.

Narrator: You know our heroine. Penelope, Antigone, Carrie Bradshaw, that girl you've been worrying about who smiles for just a little too long at your boyfriend; *(bright light flashes quickly on and off the audience)* you, yourself.

And you know her journey. *(heroine stands and takes several hesitant steps, spotlight follows)* It's a linear one that you've walked too. The stage directions guide her steps and send her to her hero. *(she scans the stage around her for hero then returns to stool)*

Maybe she'll find love after waiting years with breath bated, fighting off a hoard of suitors who assure her it's their right to assume ownership in his absence.

Chorus *(in unison)*: Her strength, we applaud.

Narrator: Maybe she'll find herself in an early grave, precluded there by her brother.

Chorus *(in unison)*: Her commitment, we immortalize.

Narrator: Maybe she'll fall for the man who promises to leave tomorrow, tomorrow, tomorrow.

Chorus *(in unison)*: Her hope, we criminalize.

Narrator: But do you know the women who dare to stand in her opposition? Don't feel bad if you missed them; they aren't the lead. *(spotlight slowly grows brighter to reveal chorus)* Their place in the thymele sits in the hollow of the hill, centered but out of focus.

They're the friend group that always looked a little too cliquey to you, but good for them. *(faint laughter audible)*

They're the sisters whose heartbreaks seem to be all they can talk about. *(faint wailing audible)*

They're the gaggle of drunk girls you meet in the bar bathroom who love your hair, love your shoes, love your vibe. Do you want to come grab a drink with them? *(chorus members visibly sway and stumble on stairs)* Oh, some other time maybe.

I think you do know them. And I think you feel their pull. *(faint harmonic humming audible)* They're the ones who sing of the murmur of bees and cling to one another, no direction but towards. Sometimes they dance. Others, they cry. Most importantly, they lean.

They lean on kitchen counters and twirl coils of phone line around their fingers while they send their hearts to one another between puffs of Marlboro Lights. *(light fog rolls out from below riser)*

They lean on shoulders and soak t-shirts between broken sobs, patting backs and holding hair through the healing. *(choral members embrace)*

They lean on one another and lean into the truth. They see through the theatrics and provide clarity to anyone who isn't quite sure what that soliloquy was all about. In their solidarity, they are separate.

Chorus *(dimly illuminated and speaking in unison)*: We are nameless, sometimes faceless; a force to be sure, but never individuals. Our message is aimed outwards, *(slight pause, heads turn as one to regard the audience coldly)* to the penny seats chewing garlic and pissing themselves. Our wisdom is passed on through rom-coms and reruns, melodrama and ballads. It's dismissed with the wave of a hand and a diagnosis of hysteria. Our gospel is filed away as gossip. *(light over* *chorus fades)*

Narrator: On stage, the heroine hears none of their insight and we're expected to see her as the lucky one. *(spotlight illuminates heroine who looks vaguely frightened as she stands from the stool)* She gets to live, and often die, for the love that we know is waiting for her. Meanwhile, they have what? Nothing?

Chorus *(in unison)*: Each other.

Narrator: Everything? But that beauty standing center stage, what would her story look like if she pivoted? If she ignored the conveyor belt that sent her into his arc and found her own? *(heroine, walking, looks down at her feet mid-step below the spotlight)*

If she stopped. *(heroine stops)* Turned. *(turns)* Redirected. *(walks slowly in the other direction towards chorus)* If she averted her eyes from the stage manager frantically waving his hands for her to find her cues and raised her chin in opposition. If she followed the spike tape that is not directly under the spotlight. If she found herself falling into the arms of her sisters rather than those of that hubristic hero. *(heroine steps onto bottom level of riser, spotlight follows her and widens to reveal entire chorus)*

What would she lose? Her glory? Her power? Her name in the credits? What would she gain?

Chorus *(in unison)*: Clarity. Companionship. Community. Support. Salvation.

Narrator: Drunk girls that she met in a bar bathroom who...

Chorus *(in unison)*: ...love your hair, love your shoes, love your soul. Do you want to come over and have some wine and talk about it we can get through this together if we try?

Heroine *(voice clear and confident)*: Oh, right now? Yes! *(stage goes black)*

Earthenware

Pandora met this place as earth and water.
A hollow and hungry thing,
ready to eat and drink from life
until she burst.

Thrown and cast in the shape of a woman
but left lacking all the substance.
Rushed centering, erected in haste.
Earthenware, porous, plastic.

Left too heavy, cracking,
bordering on bone dry but seeping steam.
Fearful of the fire, burnt to bisque,
all flaws and bubbles.

The world was happy to pass plentiful plates.
Breakfast: a bread braid of falsehoods.
Lunch: a longing larded in weariness.
Dinner: a decadent, deceitful nature.

She chewed, swallowed,
and grew.
Every gluttonous gift,
an utterly unavoidable snare.

Her wobbling walls
expanded as she ate
these ambrosial alms,
each one a source of misery.

She binged on humanity,
shoveling spoonfuls of strangers
until no space remained.
Then, she purged.

She lifted up the great cover to her jar
of a heart with shaking hands.
And she returned its contents,
each one served without consent.

Out flew endless envy.
Out flew harbored hatred.
Out flew passed-along pain.
Until only hope remained.

It fluttered there,
inside her unshakable home,
like a secret sweetness
the world never meant for her to taste.

Wave Erosion

Widow's offerings to Aphrodite have made a rocky shore of my soul. The constant emptying erodes and carves caves within me; my faults and fractures deepen each time the tide goes out.

One, two, twenty of these loves and the bedrock of my spine has warped with the pressure. Bones bent and broke as they arched to make more room still until my protective roof collapsed, leaving a sea stack that stood unguarded from all angles. In the face of such vulnerability, my love withdrew. It found a sheltering cave and grew gruesome in the darkness. Should a ship pass in the night, its captain careless enough to come close, six horrendous heads of hunger were likely to strike. This hollow place had little left to offer up, least of all an oasis away from rough seas.

I learned to loathe my love in its chamber. A new, desperate need to receive echoed off stone walls and called out to sea for salvation. Fearing for the lives of those who dared answer it, I blackened my beacons, turning inward until mine was the only siren song I heard. But the harmony held there called me closer.

It was a lonely shoreline, but one I came to claim. I made a home of that harbor, resting in my own dark embrace. The give of the damp sand beneath my feet, the calls of visiting sea birds; these things surrounded me. I gathered shells and glass rubbed smooth by tiny, crashing caresses of salt. These fragile, broken things surrounded me and shone in the sunlight, their beauty a testament to the power in my pulse.

Held weightlessly by the water, I rolled and rocked with the waves. I breathed deep and buoyant, grateful for the sun on my face. But I was empty all the same. Word spread from some Homeric Galley of the death and destruction that raged in these waters, and ships seemed to sail through any channel but mine. I felt my anatomical absence deeply and feared the day when I would cease to exist at all.

One silent night, my reflective cage was shattered by the sound of splintering wood. I watched as a sacrifice fell into the gaping mouth of another who calls this ocean strait home. Unapologetically, she fed. Spellbound, I hungered. Her ebbs and flows were enough to entice even the savviest sailor, or stranded sister.

With each break of dawn, I found myself drawn closer. I felt the contained, conflicting currents that pushed and pulled within her. I listened to her sing as the tides ripped and wrested around her. So close to my imagined solitude, she sustained herself in glory. All swirling skirts and sea foam, she was a wonder to behold.

In a rare moment of calm between us, I dared to wade my way to her. Head spinning and heart stopping, I drew breath before she drew me under. Floating in the belly of she who swallows ships, I saw the wrecks that littered her shining sea floor deep within. She held me below the surface for some time, forcing my lungs to retain what they came with.

She soon spit me out and I crashed ashore. Shivering, choking, and sobbing up salt water, I longed for another swim to her center. All flooded caves and toppling towers, I called to her until my voice went hoarse. Wading my way this time, she came. This magnificent maelstrom released the coils of herself and spread out.

She settled herself down and made a home in the hollow spaces within me, lit three-wick candles that smelled of sage and smiled in their flickering flames. She gathered driftwood in her strong arms and built a fire, right in the center of me. She placed a pot above it and made rich, endless soup. She ensured that I never missed a meal. She led me to the shoreline and washed my hair with slow hands that untied years of sailors' knots.

So, too, did I make a home in her. I learned to dive in at the first sign of spinning, left in greater awe the deeper I swam. I rode her dangerous waves with no fear of drowning. I cleared the debris from within her to make a place to rest. I rolled with her in raucous laughter on her smoothed seafloor, neither of us thinking of the noise. I painted portraits of her swirls and penned love letters to her rhythmic motion.

Over pots of black coffee, we wondered at the weakness of those unable to see the way out of a spiral; of those blind to the damage done to a rocky shore by shipwreck. Cup by cup, layers of rock and riptide fell away to reveal the silhouettes of two sisters within. Together, they jumped from high cliff faces and splashed into the sea. They danced beneath a broad moon, toes tracing spirals in the sand.

When being myself seems too great a burden to bear, she dresses me up in her. All smudged black lipstick and arms draped in bangle bracelets; I wear her like a second skin.

When the world feels too cruel to face, I hold her inside me and the walls of my cave keep her safe. Chewing a chocolate croissant and wrapped in an old wool blanket, I embrace her like a second soul.

We have not closed the passage through our shared stretch of sea. Ships are free to come and go as they please, but we no longer keep watch for approaching sails and make no efforts to quell the raging tides.

The Fall

Lilith couldn't be sure how much time had passed since she'd last been back. She ran her hand along the smooth line of moss that marked the border and it felt very much like she had been there all along. Standing, her eyes sliding from the ground where she crouched, up and into the sheltering green leaves of the trees, she felt her pulse slow.

As the breeze surrounded her, she breathed in the safety of home and went deeper. Suspended in that moment, she felt that all was right again. But there was no denying her banishment; the callouses on her soles and the bruises branching up from them served a constant reminder of the days, perhaps years, spent wandering. And still, here she was. Again and always.

It was there, in the heart of her beloved Garden, that Lilith found them. From her hiding place between the ferns, their slumber lent itself to careful examination. There was no doubt it was him. Her stomach ached in recognition of the slope of his nose; sunlight slanting off its bridge, casting a perfect triangle on his cheekbone. Her chest moved in unison with the rise and fall of his. She found the veins of his hands, a map she'd traced time and again, light as a raindrop with the tip of her finger. These parts, this whole, it was almost more than she could bear. Lingering there, where the grass curved around the arch of his hip, she was pulled back in time.

She was there with him in that same spot, ankles entwined squinting against the brightness. They looked up and looked forward to things to come. Pressing that angular nose against the flesh of her earlobe, he promised love and life and babies and magic. Breath mixing with the breeze on her neck, she felt it all. Her hand rose as if of its own accord until the back of it rested on the opposite cheek, just as his had done so many times before. Her knuckles felt the corner of her mouth lift up in recognition, a tear racing to meet it.

Tearing her eyes open, she tried instead to focus on the entirety of what she saw. But before she could stop herself, her vision narrowed again. This time, she saw the other. A new upturned palm laid next to his, so close that the two cast but one shadow.

Lilith let her eyes fall down this unfamiliar form and a new memory burned into her mind. The hair had the same mass of coils as her own. The face, with its heart shape and a fan of eyelashes resting on each side, looked much like the reflection she had come to know. The fleshy half-moons resting on ribs and the space below the navel, they matched hers perfectly. She saw what her own companionable rest must have looked like before it all changed, and it was a pretty picture.

Fury rolled through her chest like a tectonic shift, with aftershocks rising at every inch of the new body she took in. Bowing her head in recognition of the scene laid out before her, Lilith spied a serpent coiled in the grass beside her, staring up at her with the most curious look on its scaly face. She took it into her arms as a babe, whispering into the crook of her own neck where it rested. And together, they planned.

***

When the girl came to, she was baffled and amazed by everything around her. This place, at once foreign and familiar, was surely her home. It was bursting with life, and she struggled to take it all in. The sound of moving water, the birds chirping in harmony; it was music. She breathed in the smell of leaf and loam and closed her eyes to the breeze before taking stock of herself.

The two long legs below her were strong and capable; she flexed the toes and smiled as she watched their shadows dance across the grass. She pushed herself to stand, nails digging into the earth as she rose. Wiping the dirt on her thighs, she let her hands move over this body that she found herself in. The tangled tresses that caught between her fingers, the thin neck and shoulders, it all came together as she traced the length of her body to claim it; to know it as she was coming to know her home.

She looked to her side and was surprised to find that she was not alone. He was still sleeping. She looked at him lying there and felt that he, too, was at once known and unknown. His body was much the same as hers, with a few notable differences. She gazed at his face for a while, learning its peaks and valleys. His arms were laid out at his sides, palms pointed to the sky. His chest was flat and smooth, and she felt herself pulled to rest in its expanse. His lips were slightly parted, and his eyes raced behind their lids; she realized he was dreaming. She, too, had dreamt during her time in the grass but couldn't recall what she had seen. Pushing the thought away, she watched his ribs rise and fall and felt as though she were breathing in every exhale.

He soon woke and the two went about the business of getting acquainted. Hours passed in stunted words and shy smiles, the occasional light touch that sent a shiver down her spine. His hand seized hers and she yielded as he walked her around their home. As he prompted her to give names to the creatures they encountered along the way, it occurred to her that he wasn't seeing this place for the first time. They weren't exploring a new world together; he was simply showing her his.

On that long walk, she tried to learn more about her guide, what his life had been before that morning. He told her some of the things that he preferred to eat and brought her to the spot where he bathed. He told her that the song of the meadowlark was the most pleasant of all. But her questions about his dreams and the meaning of their presence in this home went unanswered. When asked how long he had lived in the Garden, or what it felt like to be there all alone, he kissed her. It had been lonely, but nothing mattered before this morning. This was the first day of his life.

They spent the rest of the day much the same, walking and talking. She was taken by every word he said. She filed away his mannerisms and facts alike, cataloging everything that he was. Her own words were slow, new, and tentative. Hand-in-hand, they walked back to the grassy place where she first woke. He laid down and gestured for her to join him. Wrapping her in his arms, he rolled over and was soon asleep.

She lay there, listening to the sound of his breathing and trying to rest as he did. But the grassy bed scratched at the nape of her neck. His hold on her was too tight and she felt a drop of sweat slide down from her temple to her jaw. Positioning and repositioning herself in vain, she wondered at his ease in sleeping beside another. Perhaps his mind was less troubled or sleep came more easily for his kind.

The girl accepted that she simply could not fall asleep in his embrace. With gradual movements, she slid from his arms and curled onto her side. The sounds of the garden at night soothed her as the insects and toads filled the air with a kind of lullaby. This time was pleasant; the cool, the silence and glorious sight felt as though they were made for her alone. Eyelids heavy, she saw a long, black snake slither up to her resting spot. It looked kind and perhaps cold, so she let it curl around her arm with its head at her neck. Together, they fell heavily into sleep.

***

Lilith watched them, the snake and the girl, as they lay off to his side. The pair dozed for some time, the crinkle between the girl's eyebrows finally smoothing in solitude. Emboldened by the night's embrace, Lilith stood to see more clearly.

He lay there with his arms outstretched but empty and she imagined the cold night air filling the space. His usually peaceful face looked tense. She thought to cast her eyes down in shame over the joy this image brought but was instantly distracted. The girl, for her part, snored quietly as she lay holding the snake in sleep. It wrapped around her forearm and found another crevice in which to rest its head. The speckles across her slight nose seemed to shine in the moonlight and a small smile pulled at her lips. The familiar angles of her body called to mind quiet afternoons spent bathing in the pond, hands slipping over skin. As the snake held this innocent interloper, Lilith, too, held her from afar.

When the moon was at its brightest, the snake woke and went down from her shoulder. Leaving the Garden and making its way towards the forest, it didn't have to turn back to see if the girl followed. Eyes still closed, her feet led her from the flowers and fruits of her nursery and into the darkness of the woods. Through the trees they went, the only sounds the quiet swishing of grass against scale and skin.

The two of them soon reached a clearing and stopped. By a large tree in the center, Lilith's words rose to meet the girl's ear. Together, they repeated an incantation in unison, "... the beauty of the Garden, the splendor of the sea, the tree, the tree, the tree..." The girl's fingers closed around the bright fruit before her, and she plucked it from its branch. Silently, she raised it to her lips. Her eyes snapped open with the crunch of the apple between her teeth and she turned to claim what was hers.

Through the trees, Lilith waited as the snake came back to her. Circling up and around her outstretched arm, it found its familiar resting place. Together, they followed their new friend as she strode back to the Garden.

***

Eve found him just as she had left him. Waking him with a caress, she kneeled, and he took the juice from her lips with his own. She half embraced him, and moonlight illuminated the single, swelling breast that met his bare skin. Down they fell, laying, coiled and knowing, bone of bone and flesh of flesh.

What comes next may be familiar to you. They had eaten that which was forbidden. They were banished and forced to roam. Shame covered them like a shroud and the world was cruel outside of the barrier of the Garden. Eve and her partner were left with no one but one another and sent off to wander. That's one version of the story, anyway.

In another, Eve smiled up into a tree at a dark, serpentine shape concealed in its branches as she led him down. She caught the eye of another, too, who was watching between low-lying ferns, and nodded in recognition. With a new knowing in her eyes, Eve passed on her corruption.

Of one thing we can be sure: that Garden is overgrown now. Without man's will and work to force it to obey, the roots have run rampant. Weeds cozy up conspiratorially to once manicured fruit trees. The path through the plots has been lost to time and Eden is but a place on earth that paints your shoes yellow with pollen. There is beauty in its unbridled bounty, and danger too. Should two women walk through its tangled mess of verdant vines, standing so close that they cast but one shadow, they are likely to be followed closely behind by a black snake, its eyes bright and curious.

Paradise Reclaimed

You can't find the Garden of Eden
pressed between Old Testament pages.
And it still isn't on any map.
But it hasn't been lost, remember?

It belongs to the little girl you once were.
The path back to Paradise waits
with her, longing for a chance to
bring back the mud between your toes.

It is dense.
And it is overgrown.
But it is there.
And it is still your home.

A misplaced queendom
where that little girl remained,
arm-in-arm with Artemis
while you were busy growing up.

Has time stolen your knowledge
of periwinkle snails kissing cattails,
and double-breasted diving ducks,
silent as they slice through sea glass?

Try not to panic.
Even addled with adulthood,
the body remembers
the subtle magic of it all.

Soak your weary bones
in an Epsom salt bath of childhood.
Let swollen knuckles ease
and bend brittle knees once again.

Again, fill your jelly jars with fireflies,
weave flower crowns in fields of clover,
and tip back heads to check under chins
for the warmth of a buttercup-cast sunrise.

For when did you last stop to listen
as Eden's echo moaned for you
on the summit of the mountains?
The sound will lead you back to yourself.

Sit as that girl consults with the daisy,
pail of plucked petals passed between you
like a sandbox scrying bowl.
She loves me. She loves me not.

Ensure her of the former.
Open your caves to her,
and when the dams have been broken,
wade with her into the river waters.

Artemis waits for you on the banks,
weak and weary from years of roaming
through the woodlands alone.
Lend your voice to her song of remembrance.

She will lead you in dances on rock edges,
help tatter your dresses and form a holy trinity
with matching pairs of quick, slick feet
and bodies blanketed in a feathered freedom.

Give in to the pull
of the milk-flesh moon.
Full and heavy, its gravity
grabs hold of your marrow.

Let lunar lanterns light your way
through trails of tall grass.
Step in boldness, without fear.
The goddess of the hunt may finally rest.

The time has come for you to take the night watch.
To slice fresh fruit to tame growling bellies.
To wipe every tear from your young eyes
and make way for summer sunshine squints.

Ease her worries with whispered revelations:
"There will be no more death,
or mourning, or crying, or pain,
for the old order of things has passed away."

You see, the path back to Paradise
begins to look a lot like love.
Like walks long and winding,
stamping Irish twin trails of footprints in the mud.

You will find yourself
taking a new way home.
Together, you, yourself,
and the smell of Eden's loam.

Reclaim for her a place of safety.
Bedtimes,
bathtimes,
and the business of binding bones.

Garden gates swing open in your absence,
ready to welcome you back with a hug,
or a fresh reminder of the hope and freedom
held in the spinning heads of dandelion fluff.

Aphrodite's Delight

Deathless Aphrodite, throned in flowers,
woke to the sound of her own growling stomach.

This was not a new sensation.

In the years since her visit with the good men,
nothing would serve to end the great pang of her hunger.

But that isn't to say she didn't try.

Aphrodite has plucked the ripest fruit
from every tree of knowledge in her city park.

She filled farmers market baskets to the brim.

Cleaned out the produce section
of all the grocery stores in walking distance.

Savored each bite, begging it to be enough.

And even tried her hand at growing
an orchard of her own for easy picking.

Still, she was hungry.

On this morning, like many others,
Aphrodite went out in search of something to eat.

But this time, it was not fruit she longed for.

This time, she retraced the steps of her sisters. Generations of starving
women followed the scent of what was stolen.

Aphrodite reached the good men's slaughterhouse.

Laid out like a buffet, she found what she craved
and pulled from her waist belt a scalloped shell sharp as steel.

Slicing thin filets of flesh from their bodies, she feasted.

Halcyon Daydreams

What if, just this once, I didn't check the weather?
Forgot to board up the windows or add oil to the hurricane lamps just in case.
Filled my kitchen with fresh fruit and left the canned goods to snooze on their shelves.
Let a daughter of wind and a son of light live in a sandcastle as close to the sea as they like.
Loved out loud as we played house and called one another Zeus and Hera.
What if, just for now, I didn't brace for impact?

I think, then, I would end up here with you.
Tracing constellations on your shoulders with my fingers as you pluck guitar strings with yours.
Waiting for the light to slant just right and set our eyes on fire.
Drinking deeply from one another and toppling over the edge.
Laughing as we chop vegetables and wondering if the tears come from onions or from joy.
I think, for us, they would come from joy.

In that life, I am not afraid of the forecast.
I race out the door at the first clap of thunder, eyes wide when the sky comes alive.
Rest my head on your wide chest, planted between the rows of potatoes, and let the storm water us, too.
Doze off with you, our bodies bindweed, watching heavy bulbs of rain bloom on dinner plates.
My mind swirls with dream-birds of calm and I float with them on charmed waves.
In our life, we are immortal.

But I fear, in another life, I have joined the Anemoi's disciples.
Awaiting the wrath of the old thunder god and preparing his pound of flesh.
Counting down on the calendar with an old red marker the end of my halcyon days.
Burrowing down deep, to hide and to sleep, and lay eggs of doubt in my nest-bed.
Shrouding myself in shipwreck scraps as my dream-clouds turn to ash and blood lightning.
But I know, in every life, I will find you.

When the kingfishers hatch, I slip away to see Somnus.
Follow murmuring waves through dusky twilight shadows and knock at the house with no door.
Seat myself by his innumerable sons and embrace the empty dream shapes.
Silently beg the mildest of the gods to fashion a shape that seems true.
Whisper bedtime stories of the light falling in love with the wind and sing lullabies of sweet summer days.
When the kingfishers hatch, I wake to find you.

Daughters of Gaia

We were born adorned in cheap costume jewelry copies of Harmonia's heavy necklace, my sisters, my brothers, and I.

They hung from our necks like a promise, or a threat. Our only inheritance.

I spent years trying to decipher what you must have done so long ago to pass this weight on to us. To me. This churning in my chest that screams for stimulation one day and begs for bones to be buried the next. You left before you had the chance to tell me the story. You tossed our lead tablet down the nearest well and fled.

More than the inescapable pain, or the blood sacrifice; more than the heart-shattering joy, or the abysmal fear, what I remember most about bringing your granddaughter into this world is the extreme feeling of injustice.

No questions asked, no background checked, I was handed her pink body in a blanket and sent on my way. How could these brilliant minds fail to see the mistake they were making? Would she not be better off placed in a basket and sent sailing down a river?

Did the curve of my spine and the fear in my eyes not tip them off? They were making a mother of a motherless child. I was expected to wipe the tears of another and lead her through the minefield that is womanhood without ever having had a guide of my own.

On the sleepless nights, I took to walking to soothe her cries. Down the dimly lit streets of our village, I whispered stories of elvan magic into her tiny seashell ears. Her cries turned to whimpers, then sighs, then sleep.

I rested by two still ponds and counted the bats that swooped overhead as she dreamed in my arms. In the silence, I came to feel myself being held in a mother's arms.

Gaia was guiding my steps, you see. She has been for years, ever since you left. Even then, the willows wept with me. Her winds gently tucked loose strands of hair behind my ears until the clouds could part and sunlight could dry bitter tears.

When the pain began to ease, she held me all the same. Her grassy hillsides cradled my resting body. They hold me still, while I write this to you. And the stars winked their pride as they told me bedtime stories.

In her embrace, I stored up the life lessons you forgot to pass on. For example, did you know that fireweed is often the first to poke out its purple flower heads after a blaze? What a lovely reminder of resilience, and the bravery that comes after destruction. The churning sand in a riptide painted my skin pink with humility; mountain peaks taught me to change my perspective, and meandering streams showed me what it is to shape the world around me.

Gaia and her girls have given me so much, Mom. I hope you know, your granddaughter will have these things, too. When Demeter ends the snowy season and Thallo breathes her buds, we will raise this child together.

They will be pleased to see our girl begin to blossom come summer, the time of fertility and growth. I just hope Auxo doesn't arrive too soon. Let the spring of youth bubble over for her a little bit longer.

And when the leaves change and fall to land at my feet, Carpo will join us in the garden. We will dig our six hands into the earth and harvest a life of gratitude. The stew will simmer on the stove and I'll set an extra place at the table for you, just in case.

Of course, the winter will return, a time to say goodbye. Demeter and I will wave to our girls from the doorway. We will rest our spotted hands and sip tea. Let the seeds lay dormant, wrapped with us in a blanket of snow.

Watching the seasons change in this way, I can't help but mourn the little girl you were. And wish I could have raised you instead. Shown you the kindness that I planted in myself to feed my daughter. Given you the gift of a dragonfly stopped to stand on water, seeing it for the first time through the eyes of a four-year-old who has never known her mother's absence. Let you drink in that special magic that you missed. I wish I could hold your young hand in mine and tell you that you never have to accomplish a single thing in order to be enough.

I mourn for me, too. And wish I could have raised me instead. I wish I could sit crossed-legged on the floor behind the girl I once was and braid her hair with gentle hands. I wish I could find the impossible strength to stick around for her.

I don't know if it was your mother, or your mother's mother, or someone long before either of them first traded love for leaving and left each new ripple to cast its own shape, but I don't blame you anymore. I just wish I could spare us both the weight of that heavy necklace. For now, I'll just be sure it never gets the chance to pass over your granddaughter's head.

A Letter to My Daughter
on the Occasion of Her 11th Birthday

My darling girl,

Growing pains are hard. I wish that I could take this cursed cup from you, but I can't; I am still working on emptying my own.

I have watched you skin your knees and shriek at the sight of your own blood. I have held you through those tears and spilled my own at the unbearable knowledge that this is only the beginning.

By now, you have probably come to see the inescapability of your hurting. That rib is raw, I know. The juice of the apple dripping down your chin and the foreign caress of the serpent, smooth scales against your skin, are not a balm to your wound.

I am surely not the first to tell you that you will have pain. And it breaks my heart that I won't be the last. As soon as you ripen, you're reminded. Your body and soul will cry tears of blood to show you how you have betrayed your purpose. And any bearing of future dissenters will rip you apart at the seams.

Constantly, you will be reminded, as if you could forget, that you will feel pain; that pain is your penance. Much of that pain will come from you, and some will come from others. But let me remind you of another truth that you mustn't forget: the scales that weigh your heart know nothing of your capacity to hurt, nor your innate ability to heal. You were born with magic spells scribed on your cells and the world can never take that away.

You may bleed. And you may birth. And you will shatter. You will betray your body and deny it many more than three times. You will present it to the world long before you learn to truly possess it. But through the blood, and the birth, and the revolution, you will take ownership. That physical pain will scar to match the broken places inside. You will scab and regenerate in ways you can't even imagine.

But I want to remind you, too, that you owe nothing to that pain. The things that hurt you do not have to make you stronger; *sometimes they just make you hurt.* You do not need to excuse unkindness because it thickened your skin or thank the gods for teaching you a lesson through suffering. In fact, my prayer today is that you do just the opposite. That your skin stays thin. That you always wear that heart on your sleeve wide open and continue to love with abandon, danger be damned.

Still, that rib will be raw. You will likely seek out ways to close the gap and ease tender flesh. After all, there is comfort in the derivative. The familiar harbor of a supporting role will stand in contrast to your inner tempest. That fractured bone will urge you from the inside to roll up your sails and let the current take you back to safety.

You must not surrender your ship. Don't let the persistent aching convince you that your pieces are not cohesive. As you come to take up more space in the world, and as it comes to take up space in you, breathe deeply. Raise your voice. Hear its echo and its significance. Feel that cage around your heart expand to make room for more. Exhale through the agony and embrace the joy to come. I promise this life is worth it.

All my love,
Mom

Acknowledgments

There are so many wonderful people who have made this book possible, and I fear I could never do them justice. But I will try. I owe you all at least that much.

Krystal, thank you for meeting me for coffee on that morning so many years ago. Thank you for holding my hand and mending my heart, time and time again. You showed me a love like I have never known. You are whatever a moon has ever meant, and whatever a sun will always sing is you.

Zooey, thank you for letting me have a hand in raising you. While I was writing my first book, you were learning to write your name. There's a beautiful symmetry in that. You inspire me every day to be brave and find the magic in this world. All the best parts of me are you and I am so proud to be your mom.

Daddy, thank you for giving me the gift of books. From teaching me to read, to getting me my first library card, to paying all the overdue book fines, to buying carts full at Barnes and Noble because I couldn't bear to be parted from my stories; you taught me to never stop learning and asking difficult questions. I miss you always.

Thank you to the friends and family who endured multiple drafts of this collection. You caught the typos I couldn't see and promised me there was a story to be told when I wanted to stop writing.

Thank you to the people whose stories are also contained within this book. I am grateful for each and every experience we shared. Even when I was less than kind in my telling of you, you loved me through it.

Thank you to every English teacher I have ever had; you all are special breed. Thank you to the one who sent me home with books above my reading level; they inspired and built me. Thank you to the one who made me mix tapes, let me grow sunflowers in his classroom window, and shared his lunch hour with me to ensure I ate something; I think you saved my life. Thank you to the one who scolded me for not wearing shoes at my dad's funeral; you were right, not cool. Thank you to the one who mentored me through undergrad; you helped me hone a craft and made college a second home. And thank you to every one who ever told me they enjoyed my writing; I hope that's still true.

Thank you to Flor Ana and Indie Earth Publishing. You were the first to give my poetry a home and I'm so glad to be on this journey with you.

And, finally, thank you to everyone who took the time to read *Reflections*. It is my heart poured out on paper. I wish I could hug you all and make you pancakes.

XO,
Azure Hall

About the Author

Azure Hall is a poet and essayist from Virginia whose work is greatly influenced by her relationship with the natural world. She studied English Literature at the College of William and Mary and lives in Cheyenne, Wyoming with her daughter, Zooey, and their cat, Valentine. *Reflections: A Mythology in Poetry & Prose* is her first full-length collection.

Connect with Azure on Social Media
Instagram: @azure_hall_author

About the Publisher

Indie Earth Publishing is an author-first, independent co-publishing company based in Miami, FL. A publisher for writers founded by a writer, Indie Earth offers the support and technical assistance of traditional publishing to writers without asking them to compromise their creative freedom. Each Indie Earth Author is a part of an inspired and creative community that only keeps growing.

www.indieearthbooks.com

Instagram: @indieearthbooks

For inquiries, please email:
indieearthbooks@gmail.com